A CONTEMPORARY APPROACH TO ART TEACHING

A CONTEMPORARY APPROACH TO ART TEACHING

Joachim Themal

VNR

VAN NOSTRAND REINHOLD COMPANY
New York Cincinnati Toronto London Melbourne

Thanks to Bea, Caroline, Frances, and Mark for their help and support.

Published in 1977 by Van Nostrand Reinhold Company
A division of Litton Educational Publishing, Inc.
450 West 33rd Street, New York, NY 10001, U.S.A.

Van Nostrand Reinhold Limited
1410 Birchmount Road, Scarborough, Ontario M1P 2E7, Canada

Van Nostrand Reinhold Australia Pty, Limited
17 Queen Street, Mitcham, Victoria 3132, Australia

Van Nostrand Reinhold Company Limited
Molly Millars Lane, Wokingham, Berkshire, England

16 15 14 13 12 11 10 9 8 7 6 5 4 3 2 1

Library of Congress Cataloging in Publication Data
Themal, Joachim.
    A contemporary approach to art teaching.
    Includes index.
    1. Art—Study and teaching (Elementary) 2. Activity
programs in education. 3. Learning by discovery.
I. Title
N350.T46   372.5'044   77-3327
ISBN 0-442-28450-0

Contents

Introduction

Children's art covers a wide spectrum—from scribble, naive, at times precocious, work, to a vast output of more or less stereotype material that is characteristic of successive age groups and serves the developmental needs of the growing child. True, valid, original art work is done sporadically by the autodidact who arrives at art through a combination of talent, instinct, innate taste, and the capacity of keeping his eyes open. More frequently it is done by children between the ages of ten to fifteen who come from privileged backgrounds, or by those who have been exposed to constructive teaching. This book is concerned with the approaches to such constructive teaching. It deals with the theory, practice, techniques, and logistics of effective art teaching, as well as with the mental, emotional, and behavioral attitudes of the art teacher and his students. The human, aesthetic, at times, magic elements of art are discussed as they relate to the development of the child.

Children and adults paint for the same reason, but not with equal concern for methods and results. Differences between their work are thus differences of degree. The cavepainter (who would be surprised to know that his work would one day be considered exquisite) dealt with a direct experience that included elements of magic—exactly as does the work of the six or seven year old. As the human embryo goes through the stages of man's biological evolution, so artists, young and old, have to discover in their own work the various stages of the evolution of art. No painter, for instance, can do honest spontaneous abstractions unless he has first worked with ideas, since abstraction is the process of stripping an idea of its concrete accomplishments. Abstraction must therefore be the essence of an idea, not its physical attributes, or be meaningless. The young are busy gathering experiences and information. The need to abstract, to distill—a form of cerebral economy, if you will—is an adult, not an adolescent need. Abstraction, thus, is not within the realm of honest children's work. Their artistic development will have only gone through some stages of the necessary evolution, and will not have reached beyond playfulness, experimentation, Sturm und Drang, concern with social problems, and, of course, sex.

What all artists, good, bad and great—from the cavepainter, the young child, and the potter who scratches a design in the clay to Rembrandt and the abstractionist—have in common, is that each will, at the outset, establish a structure, an order within which to function. The structure consists of a system, a set of rules—either conventional for a particular period or a newly invented one. All problems that arise—and they arise partly because of the particular set of rules itself—must be solved within those rules. When a child, or Klee, draws a little man with a triangular head, he will inevitably draw the next little man with a triangular head, too, thus establishing the inner coherence of the drawing, its style—predicated by, and consistent with, the medium. A painting with no rules or a variety of styles is invariably the work of an unstable person. Only very free painters get away with breaking their own rules by using a second set of rules within the same piece. This kind of true freedom may even allow them to break established personal patterns. Buckminster Fuller went a step beyond when he based his rules on the mathematical laws of nature's technology.

For the child, making up rules becomes a game. When playing the "painting game" the child does very much what he will do in life: function within a given set of rules; attempt to master life by adjusting to it.

"Playing the game" or "beating the system" is part of existing and is symbolically enacted within the four corners of a sheet of paper. (Younger, unruly, children protect themselves against their own lack of discipline by literally setting limits for themselves: before they begin a painting, they will often draw lines diagonally across the four corners of their paper).

To solve the problem of multiple motion, Duchamps invented new rules with regard to both form and content. Like a curious teenager, he kept setting up new rules and solving new problems until he decided he had solved them all, and then, he took up chess. In chess, apparently, you do not run out of problems. . . .

What Duchamps took to its ultimate conclusion—giving up painting—children will eventually do for other reasons. Problem solving is not only part of the painting game, but also part of the growth and development of the child, and there are other areas for the child to explore besides art.

If children's art is limited in time, equally limited in time is the instructor's concern for the artistic development of his student. It is the instructor's business to expose the child to the creative process, not his business to discover future artists. If any of his students *are* future artists, they will probably take care of themselves. Talent per se is, in any case, only one, and sometimes the least, of the ingredients that make up an artist. Vision, emotion, coolness, aesthetic sensitivity, conviction, (at times sheer chutzpah) and, in some art forms, a combination of some or all of these qualities with a scientific or mechanical bent, can take its place.

In the day-to-day relations between teacher and students there is, or can be, another dimension to art teaching, a dimension only implied elsewhere in this text. It has less to do with visual arts than with the experience of life and art in its widest sense.

The child's faculties—strength, coordination, mental abilities, skills—are challenged in a well-rounded curriculum where they are channelled into various activities—sports, science, social science, math, English, etc. But his senses are not acknowledged in the curriculum. The student is taught how to play an instrument, cook a dish, join a piece of wood or metal, but rarely is he told how to listen, taste, or feel a texture. His energies as related to his body and his sexuality are not dealt with, or only covertly so. The creative process is stressed in art, but aesthetics and its correlation with ethics—with honesty the common denominator—are not touched upon. Art appreciation, no matter how inspiring, is a pedantic discipline that neither deals with the orgiastic nature of art nor with its parallelism to science.

Schools (no matter how maligned) and parents are turning out a new breed of youngsters with an intuitive understanding of the basic structure of the universe, to whom technology is a living process. This new breed is ready, if their parents and teachers are not, for a world where arts and science are one; where words like beautiful and functional could be interchangeable; where the impossible is possible; where creativity, freedom, and awareness are an integral part of life.

The artist/teacher can play an important role with these children, since it is easier for him than for those involved in teaching more rigid disciplines, to introduce his students to concepts that stress the senses, the individual, even the irrational. There's nothing to it. To begin, all a teacher really has to do is to be himself: "Kids, I hate art to-day. Let's talk!"

He can play twenty questions with his students, read Edward Lear's poems aloud, write (and perform) a play with them, do psychodrama. He can ask the children to explain things to him that he doesn't understand, or take them to the nearest dump and make large junk sculptures; then cry "junk to junk" and topple them.

A teacher's freedom will infect his students. Unspoken, a seed will be planted. Persons grow on different planes at different times. The period—even the event—of incubation will differ with individual students. One of them may wake up ten years later, look at his life and his values, and decide to do something about it.

1.
Objectives and Approaches

The art teacher, setting out to determine goals for his art classes, knows that his objectives must not only be within the range of his own talents and interests, but also within range of the talents and backgrounds of his students. His first task, therefore, is to gauge the potential of his students. This potential should, preferably, be overestimated rather than underestimated: the more that is expected of a child, the more the child will give. (The converse is true, too.)

While the students' attainment of freedom and spontaneity is one of the immediate goals of the art class, the development of certain skills is instrumental in reaching that goal.

In art, however, evaluation in these areas presents certain problems. You can teach someone how to pedal a bicycle, but balance is something everyone has to *feel*. How do you measure the emotional content of a painting? Education analysts identify these near-intangibles with words like motor skills, cognitive or affective responses, etc. In art, such concepts remain fluid and personal and are open to subjective, emotional interpretations. In art, even the comparatively concrete concept of motor skill can have emotional, cognitive, or physical connotations.

Technical skills pertaining to an art activity can be learned or taught. Freedom and spontaneity cannot, but they *can* be acquired under the right circumstances. It is the teacher's responsibility to provide the circumstances that foster freedom and spontaneity and at the same time to encourage certain disciplines.

Self-expression is considered the ultimate objective of art. Free and skillful use of media facilitates self-expression. Successful self-expression, in turn, promotes a sense of achievement, confidence, and, finally, awareness. Sharpened perceptions and refined sensitivities are by-products of this process.

Before a teacher determines his objectives, he has to decide on the best method of achieving them. This sounds absurd until it is understood that it is, in fact, the method itself that determines the objective. Right methods are crucial. Right ends are rarely achieved by the wrong means. The teacher who wants his students to be free, spontaneous, and creative must himself be free, spontaneous, and creative. An ironclad list of objectives does not allow the teacher to respond freely to individual students. He therefore must coordinate his objectives and his approach.

One popular method to obtain a great proportion of acceptable paintings is to "stimulate" and "motivate" students persuasively. Although the resulting paintings do give students a sense of achievement, paintings thus produced do not fall into the category of meaningful art work. They may seem meaningful to the teacher who has successfully superimposed his own personality on that of the child. The stimulating/motivating method will, in fact, often produce delightful illustrations. These have nothing to do with art and the method that induced them constitutes a rather disrespectful—and deadening—interference with the child's psyche. (But children are surprisingly resilient and have been known to overcome.)

The teacher who would rather look for meaningful work, who seeks truth from the child according to the child's age and experience, who respects young persons, who is interested in what these young persons have to say, will create an atmosphere that is not teacher—but student-centered. He will limit his own role to that of being his students' audience—an active, demanding, enthusiastic, responsive, critical, and sensitive audience. By being that kind of audience to his students, the teacher shifts the student-orientation of his approach to the point where his presence presents a challenge and sets certain standards, standards circumscribed by his own personality. For, the teacher, too, is a unique person, not necessarily perfect, with his own ideas, idiosyncrasies, and quirks. He is to be respected, not because he is the teacher, but because he is a person, just as the child is a person. The shifting of the emphasis is all the more critical, because, no matter how student-centered his methods, the teacher cannot help being (and sometimes has to be) the dominant person in the room. A sense of humor can be one way of minimizing that dominance.

Since the teacher wants his students to draw on their own resources, to do meaningful work, and to grow in their perceptions, he will not impose his own ideas on them (as for instance by means of a lesson plan). Instead, he will look closely at his students and develop an approach that will suit both his own temperament and the talents and experiences of his students. Experience, of course, is the key word.

Firsthand, personal experience is what constitutes the raw material of artistic creation.

Since skills facilitate creativity, before any potential artist, young or old, can translate an experience into a work of art, he will have to acquire certain skills in, or at least familiarity with, the use of media (paint, clay, etc.). But even before media can serve more complicated purposes, the students should be given an opportunity to experience the sensuous, physical pleasure inherent in their use, as well as to feel the sense of power that can be derived from them.

For a child (aged five to seventy-five) dipping a brush into paint and then painting a tentative line or blotch on a piece of paper is an important experience: it gives him a sense of power. If he next uses two brushes simultaneously, holding both in one hand, with perhaps a different color on each brush, and proceeds to paint spirals on the paper, he will see interwoven spirals grow under his hands: a miracle is happening, and he is performing it! This kind of experimentation results in discovery—like finding one's first three notes on the piano. Of course, and quite naturally, the next step is to pound the piano wildly with both fists. This is where the teacher comes in: to help find more selective and satisfactory modes for further experimentation.

When the child continues to experiment and to discover and comes up with work the teacher praises (and the child has come to know that such praise is given only when meant), the child will eventually realize that he is making things that are unique, that he is creating images that are considered valuable by someone who he feels is qualified to judge.

How do such creations come about? At least a degree of self-examination will take place within the child. Self-examination is a quest for honesty. Where did the original idea come from? Should he have used blue instead of green? Each question he considers is a further step towards awareness. Awareness and growth are further developed if, at the same time, the child is helped to recognize and reject the trite, the meaningless, the pictorial cliché. He will learn that artists have to find their own language and that they have to face certain truths.

When the child finally begins to feel that what he is doing is truly his own, he will accept the fact that what he is doing is considered valuable by others. That's when the student learns to believe in the validity of his senses, to trust his own feelings. That is how freedom is achieved.

Freedom, which releases creativity, and awareness are among the worthwhile objectives of the art class in elementary and secondary schools. Basics, like design, composition, form, and color—taught to art students in colleges—are not. They are part and parcel of the education of college-level art students, and a must for the education of the art consumer. Design, composition, form, and color are subjects for which children have a natural flair, at times beautifully unconventional but nevertheless sound. This fact is amply proven by the graffiti in the New York subway system. Any mention of, say, composition, would just make children as self-conscious as that centipede who became paralyzed when asked which of his one hundred feet he usually starts off with. It would inhibit their spontaneity, as in fact, most "teaching" in art will. The wrong perspective might look perfectly right to a child one day, and perfectly wrong the next when he is a whole day older. That's when he'll ask for instruction; that's when he'll be ready to absorb it, and not a moment sooner.

The teaching of art appreciation, just as the teaching of composition and design, must be timed carefully if it is to mean anything at all. By all means, take children to museums, hang up reproductions of masterpieces (as well as of the children's own work), but don't ram art down their throats. Exposure to art is all that is needed. Children will get out of art whatever they're ready for. If they ask questions, answers should be on a personal rather than on a magisterial level. I myself find biographical data about well-known artists irrelevant. And prices? Prices should never be mentioned to American children or one will get into the wrong ball game. Art should be one area not invaded by materialism.

Involving the masters—like Rembrandt or Matisse—in an art course might lead children to assume that somehow their work is being compared to them. A discussion of Pollock would only give some children license to prolong scribbling beyond the proper age for scribbling.

Much is said about art as a formative agent. I myself plead guilty to having written on the subject in more starry-eyed days. Art will, indeed, play a part in a child's mental and emotional growth, but so will any other activity in which the child is truly absorbed. On the other hand, a child's art often mirrors and parallels the general growth of his development and perceptions at various stages of his life. In practical terms, if you look at his paintings you'll know pretty well how he's doing in English.

Though beautiful and, at times, moving work can be done with no skills whatsoever, the acquisition of skills also fulfills other very definitely formative functions. Besides facilitating self-expression and promoting freedom, the skillful use of media promotes self-discipline and gives the artist the satisfaction of technical achievement similar to the kind of satisfaction felt when a really filthy sink has been scrubbed and cleaned. A child concentrating on such an activity with accomplishment as his main incentive, will directly experience a sense of responsibility—otherwise acquired through a morality learned by rote. And a morality experienced—as an opinion arrived at—is more valuable than one accepted.

Mastering skills, of course, can also become an end in itself. This may fulfill certain needs for certain children—often the need for isolation. It can become harmful when the child becomes a showman and exploits his virtuosity as a social grace.

Mastering skills, incidentally, is also of particular importance to the creative, *new* child, product of our times, who grows up with insights, bents, and talents for science and mechanics as well as art. Such a child bridges that old dividing line between the mechanical and the artistic.

From the approaches discussed it might be assumed that the honest art teacher who wants his students to do meaningful work needs only to sit back and keep out of his students' hair. In actual fact, he will be much busier than the teacher-centered instructor who deals with, say, fifteen students as a class. The student-oriented teacher, on the other hand, has to deal with fifteen individuals, no two of whom are doing the same thing.

With the right mixture of permissiveness and challenge, the teacher will experience an upsurge of both his students' and his own creativity and encounter enough surprises to make him feel he is teaching true artists—as indeed he is—however ephemeral their careers. The actual number of children who will become professional artists later, or even who will continue to pursue their art activity after their teens, is negligible and not the teacher's primary concern. Such students are well able to take care of themselves.

While almost all children are natural artists, there are always a few outstanding ones. They will not necessarily be future artists either. Their strong response to art, sparked by a particular teacher, is usually based on a need for non-verbal communication at that particular time of their lives. They are the children who are able to form a habit of translating each new experience into a new painting.

Call it catharsis or sublimation, they have discovered a safety valve that has become a necessity for their mental and emotional metabolism. They will outgrow that need, which is not a discouraging thought. Their involvement with art will give them certain sensitivities that will add to the quality of their adult lives.

2.
Practical Aspects of the Art Room

There is general agreement among art educators that young artists should have free choice both in the selection of their subject matter and the medium in which to execute it, though the choice of the medium is bound to be influenced by what is available and by practical considerations and suggestions from the instructor.

Logically, the next step to be taken would be for attendance at the art class itself to be made voluntary. Positive involvement, important in the teaching of any subject, is crucial in art. As things stand now, the art room is a place where at given hours—say, Tuesdays from 1–2 P.M.—children are *scheduled to be creative*. Though it is manifestly absurd to schedule creativity, that is the condition with which most art instructors must deal.

Fortunately, there exist techniques that can modify the absurdity. One is to create on a physical level an environment that is both functional and conducive to concentration; on another level, to create the atmosphere of a chemical laboratory where materials and media become the catalysts of ideas, and where the student becomes the alchemist. The intrinsic interest of the whole process transforms forced attendance into participation, a "drag" into an opportunity.

The other, obvious, solution is voluntary attendance, or the open workshop. It is an alternative learning situation well worth trying to sell a principal on. One selling point for this arrangement is that such a workshop can also serve as a convenient place for other teachers to dump rambunctious, disturbed, or disturbing children. The hopefully peaceful atmosphere of the workshop will calm them. The only demands made on such children in the workshop is that they channel their aggressions into works of art—incidentally giving them what they probably need most: a sense of achievement when one of their pieces wins approval and is exhibited. The open workshop has the additional advantage that when children arrive singly, they can be set up one at a time and can receive more individual attention.

If a teacher comes to a school where an art room exists, whether attendance is voluntary or not, it is a good idea for him to move everything around. New teachers often have a rough time and aren't really accepted or established until they have gained seniority by outliving those children who were there first. By breaking up the old gestalt and creating a new identity for himself and the art room—staking, so to speak, a territorial claim—the teacher may gain a psychological advantage.

People who take time establishing themselves should not be underestimated. They usually end up by creating more meaningful relationships with their students than the smooth, less sensitive, operator who gains instant authority. "I'm new here, how do I handle this?" is not a bad question to ask of children. The authority figure, whose raison d'être is the children, thus hints at the fact of their interdependence.

When everything is moved around, the tables should be isolated so that each student can work by himself. *Art is not a group activity.* Even group murals should be simply a series of individual efforts, though peer stimulation will play a definite part in such an activity.

In the ideal art room tables should be low enough to allow a good overview while working and large enough to accommodate the materials. If nothing can be done about the tables, higher chairs will help.

Minimal materials should include postercolors with suitable flat brushes in different sizes; watercolors in pans, not tubes; and suitable round, sable brushes. Cheap watercolor brushes are practically useless; medium-priced ones are quite adequate. Grumbacher's Symphony watercolor box is best. The colors are arranged in a circle—a perfect sequence from which children will learn color relationships effortlessly. Black ink, colored inks, Yoshi reeds (rather than steel nibs), charcoal for preliminary sketches, and mat fixative are about all that is needed. The brayer used for printing (discussed in Chapter 4) is also useful for toning backgrounds with watercolor or ink. It does the job of tedious hand painting in a split second, covers more evenly, and brings out subtle, if accidental effects. Fixative doubles for unglazed ceramic sculpture. It keeps them from getting grubby, showing thumb prints, etc. Yoshi reeds are not as well known or used as much as they deserve. No school, or painter for that matter, should be without them. Yoshi reeds have an enormous range. They can be dipped in ink, into water to dilute the ink, and they can be used with a fine or blunt point. One can shadow with them by using them until the ink runs out or by applying different degrees of pressure. They can be used flat for areas, very wet for emotional work, and dry for graphic work. In other words, one can be both cool and hot with them, can practically draw and paint with them at the same time. The reeds are cheap, last long, and can be sharpened like a pencil. One child even discovered that by blowing into one end of the apparently solid, but actually porous stick, you get little bubbles at the end that throw a soft mist on the paper when they burst. "How did you get that texture!?" I said excitedly, and he showed me.

A roll of brown paper is a must, both for postercolor and black ink, and there should be plenty of cheap scrap paper in any color, plus watercolor papers in several qualities for various projects. Fluorescent (glow) colors are fun to have, but should not be used indiscriminately. They are a bit obvious and children get carried away by their sheer brilliance and use them as an end in itself. They are best used to touch up posters. Colored inks are equally seductive, but can really only be used successfully from the seventh grade up. Sepia ink, however, is a good alternative to black. Yellow and ochre inks are good for toning backgrounds. Orange ink, sprayed heavily on ceramic sculptures can dry to an antique-looking surface of bronze-like tones. Mouth-operated atomizers are useful to have, but difficult to come by in this mechanized age.

Not exactly essential, but a useful, inexpensive item to use with traditional watercolor is Mascoid, a creamy gray, rubber-cement-like medium. A labor-saving device, this resist-type medium has almost magic results when applied neatly, strong woodcut-like effects when applied haphazardly. Children often have trouble keeping watercolors evenly wet when painting backgrounds around previously drawn, perhaps complicated, figures, trees, etc. When Mascoid is used to cover the figures and allowed to dry, the whole background can be painted right over the mascoid-protected figures—even in black—with a few strokes of a wide brush. When the paint has dried, the mascoid, as opposed to other resist media, comes off by rubbing it with a finger, and the figures stand out white. They can then be treated further, shaded, painted, or left alone. Though basically a commercial medium, Mascoid is anything but slick.

Economic use of materials is important even in schools that have adequate art budgets. Respect for materials is something many children don't seem to learn at home. (I have occasionally picked up a mistreated object and shown a child what went into its making. Even a plastic ashtray has to be designed and manufactured by someone who takes as much pride in it as an artist does in a painting.)

It is a good rule not to give a child more than one piece of drawing paper at a time. If he messes it up hopelessly within a few minutes, he'll have to use the back. If he messes it up hopelessly within half an hour, he deserves another piece. Encourage a student to make sketches on scrap paper to decide what he wants to do, before he gets another piece of drawing paper. A child cannot have respect for his own work unless he has respect for the material with which he works.

It is better not to tell children how to use materials, as they'll often come up with new and interesting techniques you had never even thought of. Obviously, if they are told "this is the way you must use watercolor," they will only feel constricted. On the other hand, wasteful techniques are usually unsuitable techniques. If the child wants to paint a large area green, watercolor is the wrong medium. The answer is that he either use green paper or green postercolor. One also cannot allow a child to use a hard brush with watercolor or to pour ink directly on the paper in order to blow it in all directions. It's fun but wasteful.

If the art room has facilities for both painting and ceramics—which ideally every art room should—it is not a good idea to let children switch media in midclass. The ideal (discussed in greater detail in the next chapter) is to have the child come to the art room with an idea rather than with a particular medium in mind and to discuss it with the teacher, perhaps with sketches. The instructor, knowledgeable about media and about the capacities of the child will advise which medium is the most suitable to develop a particular idea. The answer may be an ink drawing, a sculpture, a large postercolor, or a small watercolor. If things don't go well right away the child's natural reaction will be to switch to another medium, or idea, without really pursuing the first. He may, in fact, spend the whole session floundering from one medium to another and accomplish nothing in any of them. That's where the rule of "no switching media in midclass" actually helps him. It fulfills two purposes. First, the limitation forces the student to exercise free choice by making a responsible decision, teaching him a disciplined approach to art. Secondly, it forces him to try harder, to go deeper into things.

Studies have shown that the thorough exploration of a limited number of media makes for greater creativity than the constant manipulation of new materials—often the amateur's last resort—with the medium ending up as the message.

The implementation of responsible *free choice within limits of choice* is something children respond to because of their respect for rules. Permissiveness notwithstanding, rules do help children to function, especially if the rules are explained, written down, and posted for future reference and by all means illustrated with funny drawings made by the children themselves.

If a school has a fully equipped *ceramics room*, pottery wheel and all, and the art teacher is in charge of it, my advice to him is to hold separate sessions solely for ceramics instruction.

Ceramics is a noble craft and should be taught as such. The forces that go into art sessions where skills are learned instinctively are not the same as those that go into teaching ceramic skills. Once these skills are acquired, the ceramic sculptures children will do in the art room will profit by being constructed that much better.

No child (or adult) can resist the pottery wheel and the earlier he learns its use, the better. For children, using a wheel becomes an automatic thing like balancing a bicycle; their bodies just know how to do it. It's also fun to attach paper to the wheel, and then see how circles come to life as brushes with colors are held against the spinning paper.

There is a decided tactical difference in the teaching of ceramic craft and the conduct of an art session. In art the teacher keeps away from the child while he creates, in ceramics the children and the teacher sit around the table as a group. The teacher has a different function there. He has to watch the work as it grows, come to the rescue more often, and prevent disasters before they happen.

Every phychiatrist can explain why children love to get their hands on clay. Because of their enjoyment in working with clay; children are easily and successfully blackmailed into good behavior lest they be pronounced not "ready" for clay as when they misuse it, are unnecessarily messy, or throw it around, a temptation that is hard to resist.

If there is no special ceramics room but there is a kiln in, or nearby, the art room, not a great deal of equipment is needed to include clay in the media available to students. The kiln should have an automatic shut-off with a thermostat to set it at a desired temperature. It should also be large enough to accommodate pieces up to at least fifteen inches. Otherwise, all that is needed is an oilcloth, rough side up, to cover the tables where the children are working with clay; a rolling pin; a few tools; and, of course, a sink, which no art room should be without. Even a wedge board is not essential. Banging the clay with the rolling pin as it is shaped is just as effective as banging the clay on the table, and moisture control is easily achieved with a few plasterboards that can be made in the art room with the help of the children who love making plasterboards. Most ceramics teachers make too big a to-do over air-bubbles. The myth of exploding air-bubbles should be dispelled. The fact is that if a finished piece is really given time to dry thoroughly, and fired extremely slowly, any air will escape. That's why it is important to have a kiln that can be set on low for as long as necessary. Of course, ceramic pieces must never be solid, but must be hollowed out.

White Jordan clay is best for sculpture because they can be finished in many suitable ways: spray-painted, touched up with watercolor, sprayed with a mixture of water and ink, which makes them look like granite, and waxed or shoe-polished. If the first treatment does not seem successful it's easy to cover it up with another layer of something else. Sculptures can also be burnished before firing, then rubbed with cigarette ashes and floorwax, which makes them look like old bone or ivory. They should never be glazed, because they would look cheap and pretentious.

Drying racks should be in closets, locked. Unfired ceramics should not be accessible to children. They are fragile and seem to present an irresistible temptation to destructive children.

Just as one cannot have a ceramic program without adequate storage facilities for drying sculptures, accessible storage of finished and unfinished drawings and paintings is essential, though much less space is needed. Shelves should be, if possible 25 by 30 inches, but need not be more than an inch apart. For eight classes, sixteen shelves are needed, two per class. Shelves are better than folders because they are more easily accessible. It's good for children to know their work is in a safe and special place and the teacher must know where to find work needed for exhibitions. Children should be subtly encouraged to leave their work in the art room. "Leave it or take it" usually does the trick if they know their work is being exhibited regularly. The more creative boys are usually "through" with their work once it's done and walk away from it. Girls tend to hang on to their work. They have trouble cutting the cord. Files for unfinished work guarantee continuity. Even if a child wants to start something fresh the next time he comes in, he can always return to the unfinished piece on a stale day. He's also happy when he sees that the teacher remembers his work and fishes a half-finished piece out of the file for him.

Even though the word "art" has a different meaning at the elementary level than we associate with it generally, the art experience at this level is just as important for the child as it is in later life. He learns and grows with it, develops readiness for school learning and independence in decision making.

Often there is no separate art teacher or art program at the elementary-school level, and what art activity there is must be provided by the regular classroom teacher. This situation presents special problems. Most classroom teachers use art in one form or another, if for no other reason than to give children a chance to relax between academic sessions. What actually happens in these sessions, however, is not just relaxation, but a complete change of pace. In the academic sessions given answers to given questions are expected and results are intended to be uniform. In art each child exercises his own individual forces with results that are expected to be different from those of other children.

The classroom teacher's attitude toward the use of art is always closely related to his own feelings about art, to his degree of training or non-training in art, to his private tastes, and to the physical facilities and budget that are available. For teachers who have no sink in or near their room it is almost impossible to use anything but crayons, colored pencils, or felt pens. If felt pens are used, rough paper is important. Work done with a felt pen is apt to be facile. Every artist, even a young one, needs to fight his medium to some extent.

Most classroom teachers, even those with no art training, use their sessions to the benefit of the children and seem to commit no cardinal sins, like saying, "really, that's not what a house is supposed to look like." Neither do they impose "artistic" standards on children, or get involved in criticism or corrections. They simply hang up the best or all the work and take it down again for the next batch. A few of them make the mistake of trying to get children to illustrate recently discussed academic subject matter. Designed to reinforce their teaching and to stimulate the children's imagination, it tends to turn the children off from both art and the subject matter they're supposed to learn about.

There are some ways of making classroom art more exciting even if facilities are poor and the budget small. One is to cover crayon drawings, done on white paper, with black postercolor diluted with enough water to make it flow easily. The postercolor recedes from the grease crayons (which should be applied with pressure) making the crayon appear luminous against the black. The technique has a kind of magic for the children, but overuse tends to destroy this magic. A more varied and creative technique is to use postercolor on brown paper. There are small packaged jars, six or more colors to a package, which, budget permitting, can be given to each child who can put his name on the set and be responsible for it. But the jars dry out fast if not properly closed and children are apt to use one color more than another. The teacher, therefore, would have to have a few large jars of postercolors for refills. Each child, or each two children, would also need water jars in which to clean brushes. Some of these jars will, inevitably, be spilled.

A better and cheaper way, where water jars are not needed (but which requires some effort on the part of the teacher) is to get large jars of postercolors (a few extra ones of black and white are always needed) and to fill babyfood jars with colors from them. The children, who tend to have a sentimental attachment to babyfood jars, can bring them from home. Include a few premixed colors like sky blue (blue and white), pink (red and white), instant skin (green-orange-white), and light green. Ochre should always be included in the choice of colors. It's a great color even on brown paper. Whenever someone doesn't know what color to use, ochre is probably the answer. Do not have burnt sienna. It's a dangerous color that jumps right out of the painting and vulgarizes everything. It is only good for mixing with other colors. The worst thing about burnt sienna is that, if you have it, everyone seems to gravitate to it. Van Dyke Brown is a good brown.

When the babyfood jars are filled, a table is covered with newsprint and all the jars put on one table, each with its own brush. Children should only be allowed to take one color at a time, but will, understandably, take two, and that's no tragedy. Having finished with one color, they'll bring it back to the table and pick the next one. It's important that each color have its own brush because that way no water jars are needed to clean the brushes. Depending on the size of the class, two or three jars per color may be needed, but at least not a whole set has to be made up for each child. Under the best of circumstances the colors will be quite messed up by the end of the session, but spills will be minor thanks to the size of the jars. This system also minimizes the children's tendency to pour paint from one jar to the other to see what comes out. The answer is usually khaki. It's good to hold on to it. It's a nice color that makes every color next to it look real bright.

Whether in the regular classroom or the art room, cleanliness (or messiness) can be a problem. It depends on the attitude of the art teacher, and how he handles it, whether messiness becomes a major or a minor problem. It is important that his attitude does not interfere either with the creative process or his relationship with the children. Some children, as with some adults, are tidier than others. Some are plain messy. Given the nature of the materials used—paints, water, clay—a degree of mess and the threat of disasters are unavoidable. (One of the most frequent, and preventable, causes of spills is the water jar that stands next to the artist's elbow, instead of in front in full view.) It is up to the teacher to keep the mess to a minimum by infecting the children with his own conviction of wanting to work in a nice clean room. It's okay to say, "a good artist is a clean artist," though this is not strictly true. All is well as long as the teacher is sufficiently relaxed: "Don't worry, accidents will happen. Just clean it up."

A compulsion for, or undue preoccupation with cleanliness will only make the teacher vulnerable. Children will, inevitably, respond to his vulnerability by obligingly providing him with all the disasters they think he deserves, and then some.

The well-adjusted art teacher must, occasionally, demonstrate that he himself is not above pitching in when it comes to cleaning up a major disaster. He must also make it clear that cleaning up is part of the total art session:

"You can only use pencil and paper today."

"Why?"

"You left a mess last time and we had to clean it up for you."

Children who are constitutionally messy will have to work with similarly antiseptic materials until they make a visible effort to be neater. It will help teach them self-discipline which is part of growing up.

Time should be allowed for the clean-up at the end of each session and the process should be structured in a practical manner that makes sense in relation to the physical set-up of a particular room. A step-by-step approach is essential to make the clean-up manageable for children: for example, all waterjars to be removed first, all brushes collected next, etc. One child could be appointed to be in charge of issuing materials in the beginning of a class and to supervise and help with the cleanup. If the child relates well to the teacher, perhaps even emulates him, he might not even bully anyone.

3.
Teaching Responsively in a Structured Class

Student: "What shall I do?"
Teacher: "How should I know?"
Student: "I can do what I want?"
Teacher: "Of course."
Student (looking around): "Can I use the same stuff he's using?"

Children are flexible. This one, though perhaps accustomed to the "now-children-remember-our-visit-to-the-zoo" school will rapidly adjust to a new approach. Most seventh-grade students, of course, have already been exposed to art in some form or another. Some will know all about art, others will be locked into stereotypes, i.e., the child who faithfully reproduces figures from comic books and cartoons. Some may have the automobile fixation, others, the dynosaur syndrome (a characteristic of children with emotional problems, who find reality unpleasant, perhaps unbearable). The teacher must find techniques to guide such students into new areas, perhaps find at first a more creative context for their favorite motif, or help them discover alternatives that are within their range. However, timing in such cases is a delicate matter where teaching can turn into meddling, and some children (particularly the ones with dynosaur syndrome) may be best left alone. Children, especially in art, learn as much or more from each other as from their teacher and it may be more fruitful to let that process take its course. All this is easy when dealing with individual children who arrive one at a time.

The individual approach, basic to any meaningful art teaching, is just too time-consuming when an entire class comes to the art room at one time, and for the first time at that. The teacher either stands at his desk and gives each child, as he comes in, a few sheets of paper and ink, or whatever simple material he wants him to use, or lays the materials on the tables ahead of time.

After the class sits down a brief speech is useful where points that a teacher finds important can be stressed. Perhaps like this:

"I'd like to have an idea what you can do. You can do anything you want. Don't try too hard. Relax. If you don't know what to do, doodle.

If you don't want to do anything, don't do anything, but don't disturb the others. Don't work fast. Work slowly. Try to stay in the middle of the paper. Keep away from the edges."

For the first class, papers should not be bigger that ten inches square and each child should have a few pieces in case of miscarriages. The first day is not the day for calculated stinginess. After a while the teacher goes around and sees what the children are doing. That is the scenario. Watch the expression on the children's faces. Some will be utterly absorbed in what they are doing. Don't go near them. They don't need you. Go later and you'll be surprised. By the time the teacher has made his rounds and has seen what the children are doing or have done, he has a pretty good idea of where they stand, and, up to a point, can gauge their potential.

Once the shock and panic of the first class in a new school has worn off, it is of the greatest importance that a teacher *sets the tone of his class or workshop at the beginning of each period by making a ceremony out of the issuing of the materials.* This opening ceremony should become part of the structure of the art session—like the organized cleanup at the end of the class.

By this time, the children, too, may have a pretty good idea of where you stand. Where *do* you stand? You have a great conviction about art. You see a potential artist in every child that comes to your room. You know it's up to you to find his forte if he has not found it yet. You know that there are no two children that have the same problem. You endeavor to imbue each student with the seriousness of his undertaking. You therefore begin each class on a highly professional level by having a miniconference with each student and by making a formal ceremony out of the issuing of material that is most suitable for his particular project, a process that involves both his and your own creativity. Sometimes, special materials are not just given but *conferred* upon a student:

"Look at my sketch! I want a big piece of paper."

"Wow! Watercolor?"

"Yeah!"

"Wait, I think I have a few pieces of that really fancy paper left. Here. Here you are."

"Thanks!"

"What are *you* going to do?"

"I dunno."

"Here's scrap paper and charcoal. Sit down, doodle, and make up your mind. I'll look at it later."

"George! You started that picture with those weird figures. It's in your file. Take watercolors. Wait. Here. I think that's the brush you need."

"What about you?"

"I have an idea."

"Yes?"

"I can't explain it. Can I have white paper and ink?"

"Here you are. Don't get it all over you."

"Yes?"

"I want to make a spaceship in outer space."

"What about postercolor on black paper? Then you don't have to fill in the black for the space."

"Yeah! Can I have glow-color?"

"If your picture comes out good I'll let you have some for last touches. Okay?"

"I did this last week. How shall I finish it?"

"Garbage cans? Doesn't seem very exciting."

"*You* sent me outside to draw them."

"I know. I wanted to get rid of you. You were fighting with Diane. But you know? If you'd use all the wrong colors, it might make it very interesting."

"Like neon-red lids?"

"Why not. Yes?"

"Shall I use all the wrong colors on this, too?"

"Let me see. No. Before you do anything, make three tiny identical sketches. Then, just in black and white, try out different ways, like white background or black background, and see what works best. It'll give you ideas of how to do the whole thing in color later."

The better you know your students, the better you'll be able to help them make choices. Choices is the key word. It develops their capacity to think for themselves. Spontaneity and freedom have been advocated in previous pages, but they are only the first step. Those small sketches where alternatives are tried out, also have to do, on a higher level, with that sense of "power" discussed earlier and the sensitive teacher will know whether the child is mature enough to bring other qualities to his work - like thought, and the ability to make choices—deliberate, intelligent choices of materials, ideas, and ways of developing a piece of work. Based on what is available and on his knowledge of the child's abilities, the teacher may spark this process by suggesting something the child has used before, but not yet fully explored, or something new and entirely different. For the more experimental child sometimes the medium itself, rather than a pictorial idea, can be the point of departure.

One thing a teacher has to keep in mind is that a child's approach to painting should always be step-by-step, the approach used in most other learning situations. When an adult painter begins a painting he may be able to deal simultaneously with composition, color, design, expression, and the materials themselves. A child certainly cannot handle the total approach and must be set up in a way that allows him to handle one problem at a time. This may well include drawings to be colored in later, considered a despicable, "color-me-pink" technique by some. It can be reversed by painting first and later articulating the painting with pencil or ink.

Unsuccessful paintings can often be saved *by washing them off,* even scrubbing them. It's quite a creative pursuit at that. Children enjoy the subtle transformation paintings undergo under the running faucet. Overpainted pieces, particularly, may only need to be touched up in a few places after the water cure. I remember a well-trained ten-year old, wise to the ways of the art room, holding up his latest masterpiece and asking; "Is this ready for the sink or the garbage can?"

The emphasis on slowness was made earlier for a very good reason. Somehow, a line drawn slowly conveys more meaning than one drawn in haste, just as a piece of clay, endlessly smoothed by a child, will by some miracle reflect the love that has been brought to it. As to telling children they don't have to work if they don't want to, this is, of course, sheer bluff: I've yet to see the child who can resist a blank piece of paper. On the other hand, for children already well into the artistic process, sitting before a blank piece of paper can be an awesome responsibility as well as an adventure. Throwing a stone into a quiet pond, to destroy purity by pressing charcoal against white paper is, at first, to violate. Such violation, when it is not vandalism, can become an act of courage, a risk, a decision for change, a responsibility. This is where art becomes growth: we are answerable for what we do.

It was earlier suggested that children should keep away from edges. One only has to look at the rhythm and elegance of New York subway graffiti to know that the young have an instinctive feeling for design and composition. Asking them to keep away from the edges will not only save them from pitfalls, but will channel their creativity into a manageable format, i.e., will structure it. There's another, very practical consideration. What happens to paintings that go right to the edges when one wants to frame them? Traditionally, watercolors and drawings don't really have to look finished, while postercolors and acrylics usually are painted to the edges. (I do not mention oils, since I do not feel they are a suitable medium for school children. They are messy when not handled carefully. Oils also need the kind of purposeful planning that contradicts the whole premise of children's art. Unlike more casual media, oil painting is a kind of commitment, and can even be pretentious.)

The size of paper used by children at different stages is important and requires a great deal of understanding, sensitivity, and foresight on the part of the teacher. When projects are discussed, sizes should be discussed, too. Paper, which comes in standard sizes should not just be handed out as it comes. When necessary the teacher should involve himself in the cutting. Ripping the paper by means of a tightly held metal ruler does the trick in a split second and the slightly uneven edge is more attractive than the straight cut of a blade. The direction of the paper, which hardly ever comes square (but sometimes should), will usually be decided by the child himself. At times one has to use foresight: "Better turn the paper. You'll never get the feet in." The alternative is to attach another piece of paper to the first, to get the feet in. Younger children of both sexes will use paper horizontally, but boys will one day turn it to a vertical position as they grow more mature. I usually hide a smile when I see that day has come. Adult students, too, when starting a painting, often have a problem deciding whether they feel vertical or horizontal that day. I have an entirely unconfirmed theory that vertical paintings are statements while horizontal ones tell a story.

There are schools of art teaching that advocate "large" pieces of paper for all children, a practice that, if applied indiscriminately, will, in my opinion, lead to sloppiness, emptiness, poverty of content, unresolved work, and storage problems. Painting large is good when in conjunction with body movement. In a free art room any child can get up and paint from his elbow if he wants to. Children who like to work small will eventually come around to using bigger areas as they gain self-confidence. Occasionally you come across a youngster who does well with large pieces. Such personal need to create a sizeable reality can be caused by a vision that refuses to accept limitations, but also by a certain infantilism. Generally speaking, though, children are scared of large surfaces that are difficult to manage and demand to be filled. Of course, subject matter, medium, size of brushes, and composition are all closely related to size. Each painting, in fact, seems to have its "right" format. Occasionally one comes across a painting or sculpture, whether by a child or a professional artist, that's just not right—until one realizes that it ought to have been bigger—or smaller, just as one finds novels that ought to have been short stories or short stories that should have been expanded into novels.

Each child will present a new challenge. One has to guess where he wants to go, where one feels he should go. Sometimes it's just a question of helping him to go the whole way. This is an important concept. Once in a while you come across books, films, and plays where the author failed to carry out his idea to its fullest; it fell short somewhere. In art teaching on any level, it is the instructor's job to help his students to take an idea, a composition, to its ultimate conclusion.

Children who do not know what to do should be left alone. Let them be bored. They won't be bored for long. Boredom is often the prelude to creativity and invention.

Obviously, recipes for what to tell given children cannot be specific. Where specific specifics are given, they are given against our better judgment. Recipes merely inhibit a teacher's creativity functioning in response to the student's creativity. Such a condition of mutual inspiration is sustained by the instructor's infectious enthusiasm for, and belief in, art.

Each child is an individual, but there are always a few who fall into predictable categories. There will be those who need you merely as a responsive audience or consultant. Either naturally, through previous teachers, or through their cultural background, they are already where you want them to be. When you see what they are doing don't be afraid to say "wow" if you feel wow. Discuss their work with them professionally as you would with a college student or adult painter. Tell them where you think their work is weak or could be better. Maybe you see, somewhere in a painting, the point of departure for another piece. Tell the student.

There'll be the conscientious intellectual student getting frustrated trying to do something beyond his abilities. Don't show him how to do it, unless he asks specific questions. It won't do any good. He'll get there, eventually, on his own. Give him another piece of paper, tell him to doodle, to switch off his brain, or to close his eyes while he draws. He must first learn to relate to the paper, become familiar with the use of materials per se before he can use his intellect in art.

Personally, I wince at clichés, whether pictorial or verbal. A reliance on clichés stifles growth. Clichés are the result of not thinking for oneself. They often result from a narrow cultural background in which ideas and stereotypes are accepted without question. A child who grows up in an environment that is cliché-ridden, restrictive, or banal will do work that is derivative, stiff and unfeeling, or "cute." He has to be led, sometimes shocked, into thinking for himself and into saying what he wants to say.

There are seasonal clichés that are difficult to combat, like those used for St. Valentine's Day and Thanksgiving. I once laid down the law before Thanksgiving and said I'd scream if I had to look at another turkey. Among the results: a beautiful abstract variation on the theme "turkey," a good piece of work in its own right; and a drawing of turkeys sitting round a table that held a garnished platter containing a pilgrim with an apple in his mouth. Though I disapprove of artists who try to be different and original at all cost, I liked that pilgrim.

Another recurring phenomenon is the child who, conditioned by "bang-bang" comic strips, faithfully reproduces cartoon images, replete with written dialogue. He should be induced to tell the story in pictures only. "Either the picture isn't good enough, or you think I'm too stupid to understand it." If you encourage the child to try new media, to work with areas instead of lines, and to think in new contexts, he may eventually give up cartoon drawing for more original work, but such habits are often hard cases to crack.

There are several ways to deal with faltering students who seem to be at sea with your approach. They have to be introduced to the simple enjoyment of the act of drawing and painting, given a chance to experience that sense of power discussed earlier. One of the simplest cures for the anxious, rigid student is to give him a wet piece of white paper. If the student touches it with a reed, brush, or pen dipped in ink, the ink runs! If the class is large, call other similarly inhibited children to watch and they'll all want to try it and see how the ink comes to life on their paper. It's a good trick, but wears off and can, at that stage, become sterile. Another technique with similar drawbacks but which almost always guarantees effective results is to cut a form out of a piece of cardboard, and then to put both the cut-out form (positive) and the cardboard from which the form was cut (negative) on a sheet of white or colored paper. Black or colored spray paint is sprayed lightly over the cardboard pieces. The negative cut-out will result in a dark form, the positive in a (left out) light form. The pieces of cardboard are then moved into different positions on the paper and sprayed again. Blended by the spray paint, the results are kind of slick but dramatic as long as the child is stopped before he gets carried away (or begins to direct the spray at living targets). Alternate sides of cut-out cardboard forms, especially if figurative, can also be used under paper to make rubbings that can be left alone or worked over in different ways. All such indirect "mechanical" techniques are good to start children off. Although their effect wears off, these techniques should remain in the teacher's repertoire because they will come in handy again later when the children are ready to do more sophisticated work, involving mixed media, controlled accidents, etc.

Another trick is the doodle, mentioned frequently in these pages. The doodle really deserves a book all its own. The idea of the doodle is to release forces that will eventually permit the child to draw on his own personal experience for his creative work.

First hand, personal experience is the raw material of art. In our mechanical age, our pushbutton existence, many children's experiences are almost entirely relegated to what they see on television and in the movies. Little they can actually do will be as sensational as the events they can turn on and off on the TV screen. Even the adventures of Jungle Habitat, Disneyland, etc. are safe, mechanical, and well-organized. Since part of the creative act consists of organizing chaos, what can be done, creatively, with something that already is organized? Thus the young artist has to rely on his inner experience to produce work that is his very own and finds its meaning in intangible qualities that can be found nowhere else.

Though it may, at first, be purely mechanical the doodle will say something about the doodler, just as handwriting—and everything else one does—says, or hides, something about the writer. It may show one aspect of a person or merely a typical one. It may show the story of his life.

Doodles can also be stereotypes. They usually don't come fully developed, but have to be cultivated. In art teaching the doodle can become the microcosm of art itself.

For the purpose of the art teacher the doodle is the ideal device to get students started. Since doodles are mechanical, playful, and kind of silly, they are not much of a commitment for the anxious student who is afraid to expose himself. It is an easy beginning for anyone. And it may carry the germ of a painting. To develop this germ, the instructor's ingenuity is essential.

If a child makes a perfectly banal stick figure, sit down with him. Suggest that he repeat the figure a few more times, put some upside down, fill the paper with them, some big, some small. If the figures are done in ink, show him how to roll different watercolors over them with a brayer, or suggest that he put blobs of color on each one. Hold up his work. Show him what he's done! Suppose his doodle was just a spiral. Tell him to make another spiral next to it but in the opposite direction. Presto, you have two eyes. Add a nose, a line for the mouth, put a circle round it—and you have a face, or an owl. Color it blue. He could also have colored the original spiral, put a square around it and a circle round the square and colored it green and blue. The possibilities are endless.

It can be argued that such a set-up piece, developed at the suggestion and under the guidance of the teacher, is meaningless, even if it ends up looking like a sophisticated Klee. It is, by itself. Its purpose is solely to open up new vistas for a child accustomed to thinking of art in terms of what he has seen at home and in museums—something forbidding, an accomplishment beyond his reach. Suddenly he's told that all those stickmen look like something, and he can see that they do. He realizes how simple it is just to fool around. That one single experience may have freed him. The teacher's battle is won once a child's appetite for experimentation has been whetted. He'll go on from there. He may even develop the habit of doodling, become so free in it that the doodle will spring directly from his subconscious and tell as much as symbolic dreams. One of my own doodles, no bigger than an inch, was a small figure with a kind of tire round its neck. I soon realized what it meant. I had been stuck in a situation of sudden responsibility which I both liked and resented. The figure was myself, the tire really a "millstone round my neck." (The subconscious is notorious for using clichés.)

Once a teacher has established himself as a person with strong convictions and sincere interest in his students, he can become more and more demanding. As mentioned earlier, the more that is expected from children, the more they will give. He will even be able to afford to be quite honest with them. If, on his rounds, the teacher sees something that is terrible, he can laugh and say "it's terrible." Children are often conditioned from kindergarten onward to receive indiscriminate approval for everything they concoct. In their hearts they suspect that teachers are either outright dishonest or afraid to discourage. Since praise has thus become meaningless to them, an art teacher who is direct and says something awful is awful comes as a refreshing surprise. Above all, it means that when he says "it's great," the child can believe that what he has done really is great.

Honesty with students is an essential ingredient of an art class that aims at honest work. It's just another kind of brainwashing, if you will. Honesty is contagious. Children instinctively detect phoniness and instinctively respect straightforwardness. They also like to know where they stand, as who doesn't! Besides, being dishonest towards young persons is being disrespectful of them.

Being honest, of course, does not give license to be rude or insensitive for the sake of honesty. When you know that a particular child has limitations and cannot do better, you don't tell him his work is poor. There are always ways and means to set a child to doing something that will satisfy both of you. There are even cases where you can, if necessary, violate your own cardinal rule, never to touch your students' work.

The art instructor who deals with the pictorial cliché only deals with one specific aspect of a wider problem—how to deal with those sensitivities that, lacking a better word, we will call, reluctantly, "good taste." I use this nomenclature reluctantly, because the very words good taste evoke a miasma of snobbery, presumption, and putdowns, not to mention controversy. The very people who profess to have good taste (which, if anything, reflects a quality of restraint) are at times excessively ostentatious about it, thus negating their claims (like the purist who either will not have a television set in his home, or hides it behind austere paneling). It is, actually, a personal matter for each teacher to decide whether it is even a problem he wants to address.

The controversy is really caused by a semantic confusion. Actually, good taste non est disputandem, because it is a constant, while it is "taste" that changes with people, seasons, centuries, or cultures. On matters of "good taste" there is, and always has been, a complete consensus.

As it happens, the question of good taste could almost be ignored since it does not come up except in its violations. If it has to be brought up, it is because it involves attitudes crucial to art in general. The art teacher will encounter only a limited number of examples that actually fit into the category of insensitivity, bad, or poor taste (usually covered by words such as thoughtless, derivative, sentimental, cute, obvious, phony, pretentious, and excessive. Obscenity is rare among children, though there are instances of excessive Freudian frankness).

The German language has a word for it: kitsch. It covers part of the same problem, is kind of humorous, yet deadly, can be modified by saying, "a little bit on the kitsch side," which would make the object under discussion only a little bit too cute, sentimental, coy, sugary, tawdry, or obvious.

A fact the instructor also has to keep in mind is that the sensitivities that go into what we call good taste are subject to evolution. Today's art connoisseur was not necessarily born with instant discrimination. He may have loved kitsch at one time in his life, just as the humanitarian of today may have tortured animals during his childhood. It's perfectly all right to like the wrong things before learning to appreciate the right ones. The wrong things were perfectly right at the time, perhaps even necessary. But it's rough for the dedicated teacher to stand by hoping for bad taste to go away rather than trying to help a particular child in his development.

In some cases, criticism must be held back or well-timed, especially when excesses occur during the period when the child revolts against rules and conventions in order to establish his identity.

Truth is the common denominator of good art. Truth coupled with intense emotion can become magic art which children are quite capable of producing. Nobody will apply standards of good taste to Mayan or African art, no matter how phallic, or to Francis Bacon's or Goya's work. But put an airport-art-type African imitation next to the genuine piece and you have a stereotype that is not only meaningless and blah, but more closely related to the ten-year old's St. Valentine's heart than to the African piece it pretends to be. Such products are the result of thoughtlessness and cross-cultural confusion. We cannot provide roots, but we can help students to focus and think.

Developing sensitivities like truth and feeling in students is not just a task for the art instructor, but belongs to education in general. The social and ethical values of these civilizing qualities will be carried over from childhood into personal attitudes of adulthood, even if in a quite different creative outlet.

Viktor Lowenfeld has more or less established a time table for the creative changes in the growing child, as Piaget did for the psychological stages. However, the differences in creativity of boys and girls, or, more precisely, in their *creativity and attitudes at different age levels*, is a subject ignored in curricula. It is not a subject which I'm prepared to tackle in all its physiological and psychological implications, but which I will discuss in relation to my own practical observations. Conclusions such as these are bound to be conditioned by the experience a teacher has had with class sizes, boy/girl ratios, socio-economic and racial constellations, etc., as well as by the teacher's own sex and sex attitudes. They may nevertheless sharpen the reader's insight into different stages of a child's development, and may even help him to think up appropriate methodologies to deal with them under specific circumstances.

I find that boys and girls are equally creative and have the same approach to art until they are eight or nine years old, and again in their late teens, but that they diverge greatly in the intervening years. Since persons, young or old, refuse to conform to their chronological age, one cannot pinpoint exact ages; but by the age of eight, nine, or ten girls seem to handle their growing awareness entirely differently from the way boys do. They become self-conscious about their work, very self-critical, won't believe you if you praise their work, but will also resent criticism. Their work often becomes conventional (flowerpieces, still lifes) and repetitive (safe). Their emotions, instead of being used in, and contributing to their art work, seem to get in their way. During this period a teacher has to use all his ingenuity to reassure them, to challenge them, to think up new projects for them. The same girl who flounders in a drawing may perform beautifully with colored paper and scissors, a collage being, somehow, a less threatening, more tangible, solid thing. This is part of the subtle change in approach: quite often pragmatic projects, like a ceramic bowl that can later be used as a present, may be the answer. While there are girls who, unaffected by changes, will continue to be productive and creative during this period, for others full creativity may not come back until they are sixteen or seventeen.

Almost, but not quite, the same years that are so difficult for girls are the years of discovery for boys. Between the ages of ten to fourteen boys are still sufficiently uninhibited to be direct, still naive enough to be sincere, and not yet ashamed of their feelings. This is the time when their awareness and intelligence are awakened, where they are eager to absorb new insights, learn new points of view, and try to come to terms with reality. In contrast to girls of the same age, they are not only not critical of their work but are inclined to love anything they do. They also begin to take pleasure in their manual dexterity: their hands begin to actually do what their eyes tell them!

This is also the time when girls have crushes on their teachers (not always easy to handle), and when boys identify with, and emulate their teachers (which can be ignored). Not that easily ignored are those boys who pick this time for a perfectly healthy rebellion as part of their perfectly healthy development (discussed further in Chapter 8 on teacher/student relationship).

Partly because of new interests and partly because of peer pressures, by the time a boy is fourteen his art activity tends to become intermittent, or, at least for a while, to end altogether. This is likely to happen even in a well-established art program. There are, of course, schools where certain social pressures are so strong that a new art program has trouble getting overall acceptance in the first place. In such schools, where sometimes the children are not the only ones to blame, it is not until teachers and students alike cease regarding art as sissy that the art program will really become respectable. How soon that will happen can sometimes be influenced by the art instructor's own attitudes. Often the art program does not gain respectability until the right children—those that are also good in sports—become interested in it.

There does exist one particularly useful area where the barrier between arts and sports can be broken down, namely in the making of *posters* for special school events. Some instructors resent the demands made on their time and on the facilities and resources of the art room, especially because such demands usually arrive as rush jobs, in almost crisis situations. "You are having a baseball game? I've heard of baseball. How do you play it?" obviously is not the most helpful attitude to take.

Actually, the making of posters is an art in itself. Posters, having very different objectives, offer very different techniques from regular art work. Since anything goes in a poster, including the use of cutouts, caricatures, photographs etc., a poster is a challenge and an exciting project for children of almost any age. There is no reason why the class that happens to be in the art room at the time the request for posters is made should not get involved in the project. It is also good strategy to show the athletes themselves how to make kinetic drawings of themselves in action and to direct them in the use of colors, black and white, and effective lettering. This might also be the time for the teacher to overlook his own "hands-off-the-kids'-work" approach and become actively involved himself. The public showcases usually reserved for art work should in such cases be given over to these posters, especially if their quality and execution are a credit to the art program.

4.
Reversing the Image

"Can I have a piece of linoleum?"

"You're too young. You don't have the coordination to use cutting tools."

"Yes, I do."

"What does 'coordination' mean?"

The child holds up his two fists and moves them as if he were driving a car: "It's when your hands . . . ."

A child will understand the meaning of an abstract word when he's ready for its concept. This one is.

Linoleum cutting is popular with teachers, and rightly so, but does not make much sense until a child has some degree of coordination. If the child's physical development conforms to his chronological age, coordination usually comes when he's ten or eleven. He won't however, really excell at it until he is older, which is why the printing medium occupies an elite position among the media used in the art room.

Linoleum cutting at its lowest level, as practiced in kindergarten, consists of cutting holes into the surface of a piece of linoleum, rolling ink on the surface, and then pressing the linoleum onto a piece of paper. Where the holes are, the paper stays white. The resulting print provides a certain I-caused-that-effect thrill in the child. Since the image is reversed and carries a surprise element, it becomes something that is both brand new and familiar. Since the result is achieved indirectly and by mechanical means it also carries a certain rightness where you don't question the result, a *finality* even for those who always see flaws in their direct work. Special emphasis is placed on the word finality because that quality is an important ingredient of the printmaking process. Its indirectness, the resulting finality, as well as the surprise element in the actual printing, all play a part in the fascination printmaking has for children and adults alike.

Very much like the ceramic process which has a creative and a mechanical phase—the forming and the firing—the printing process also has two phases: designing and cutting the block and the actual printing. And, just like ceramics where one is never quite sure what will be found when the kiln is opened, one never knows what the print will look like when peeled off the block.

Unpredictability (which is the spice of life) and the controlled accident can become part of the printing process and can be developed into a creative and exciting activity.

CUTTING THE LINOLEUM

Needed for Phase I are pieces of linoleum in suitable sizes. Art stores also sell linoleum in sheets that can be cut up. To cut linoleum, put a ruler on the burlap with which the linoleum is backed, slide along with a blade, then simply break at the cut. Linoleum also comes mounted on blocks of wood. These precut blocks are more expensive but easier to work with. If straight linoleum is used and a print turns out to be very successful and might be used repeatedly, the linoleum plate can be mounted on a block of wood. The linoleum comes with some kind of grease on it and this has to be removed with water and scouring powder before it will accept ordinary paint.

Cutting tools come in two types, push and pull. The pull-type tools (Linozip) are safer and easier for the child to control. The child holds the linoleum with one hand and cuts away from it. When he slips, and slip he will, he will not cut his hand. Who am I kidding? Of course he'll cut himself, so the art room must be stocked with disinfectant and adhesive bandages. Keep a few discarded pieces of linoleum on hand so students can practice and get the feel of working with it before they start cutting the designs. If the linoleum is warmed for five minutes on the radiator, it cuts more easily.

Before discussing the technical aspects of the printing medium, it seems worth mentioning that in spite, or because, of its severe technical restrictiveness (as compared to other media), blockprinting has a way of accentuating in each child the creative "type" to which he belongs, and which Viktor Lowenfeld describes as visual and haptic. According to Lowenfeld in *Creative and Mental Growth* the visual child works "as a spectator, with his eyes as intermediaries for his experience." If this type wants to draw, say, a basketball player he will draw him the way he can observe him from the edge of the court. Lowenfeld feels the haptic artist (from the Greek *hapticos*, for "able to lay hold of") is primarily "concerned with his own body sensations and subjective experience in which he feels emotionally involved."

This type will think how it feels to jump for a ball then draw that bodyfeeling kinetically. This is also the child who, asked to show how he would jump, jumps and suddenly will know how to draw a jump.

I'm inclined to add a third type, product of our technological age, and no less creative: the child who likes to solve visual-mechanical problems and takes particular pleasure in his manual dexterity (more about this third type below when the actual printing process is discussed).

Though there is evidence of Lowenfeld's two creative types in the work of all children, nowhere do children seem to be channeled into those types more tightly and obviously than when they try to express themselves through the printing medium. It is as if the young artist compensates for the restrictiveness of the medium by emphasizing his individuality. At first glance this seems to be a contradiction: Permissiveness facilitates freedom of expression, but restrictiveness can also. I'm not sure what actually happens there.

The two types, as it happens, attack the problem of cutting or designing the linoleum cut in radically different ways. The haptic child will cut directly into the linoleum, without previous design. He takes pleasure in the physical act of cutting as an end in itself. Some, perhaps inarticulate children, may cut clumsily and awkwardly, yet come up with prints that are eloquent in their emotion.

The visual child designs the print before cutting. For him the actual cutting is a chore that must be done in order to achieve certain results. Since the image will be reproduced in black and white, and reversed, any child will at first encounter difficulties, like having to write his name backwards. A mirror will be needed to check mistakes. (Every art room should have a few mirrors. They are needed for self-portrait. It's also good for a child to look at his work in the mirror. The reversed image gives him a different perspective of his work and a more objective judgment.) The child cutting the print will have to adjust to its reversal, just as the photographer must be able to "read" his negative. There is no point in telling a child these things; he has to find them out for himself. He will soon learn that the line in the linoleum is exactly the opposite from the line made by the familiar pencil: in the print it will become a white line instead of a black one. So, if he wants a black tree, he will have to leave the tree and take away the surrounding area. Only after the child has discovered for himself what he cannot do, can the instructor set him up in a more foolproof way: the linoleum, which usually comes in gray or white can be painted with black ink and the drawing done with white poster-color over the black. The brush used should not be too thin. A fairly thick brush forces the child to adjust his design to the brush (and indirectly to the other medium). He will not, therefore, use details that will be beyond his ability to chisel out of the linoleum. His white design on black will appear the way the final print will appear, except in reverse and without the certain charm that the linoleum-cut medium possesses. Another method is to make a careful ink drawing on the linoleum, then whiten or blacken in all the areas that will later have to be cut out. Through this step-by-step approach, the actual cutting job will become more or less mechanical, which it should be. At times, a natural division of work will develop among the children. The artist will design the print and the mechanical child will cut it.

PRINTING

The physical requirements, mechanics, intrinsic fun, and productivity of the actual printing process make it, indeed, a phase all its own, and an independent activity in which practically every child in the class will want to get involved. Since all available surfaces of the art room will probably be needed, it is a good idea to set aside a special session just for printing.

The children will have cut the linoleum blocks in regular art sessions, during which, however, it is not practical to set up cumbersome printing equipment. The best they can do then to find out whether their cut is successful, is to make a rough trial print with postercolor on towelling.

To set up the room for a mass-printing session, large tables have to be used or smaller ones put together. Materials needed include: a few large pieces of glass or acrylic plastic, brayers in different sizes, special printing paper in different weights, and printing ink. With printmakers proliferating all over the country, art stores carry a wealth of suitable printing papers that range from inexpensive papers of good quality to more costly oriental papers, some of which are almost transparent, yet tough, and so beautiful to behold that it is almost a shame to print on them. Black and sepia inks are needed, plus colored inks in your favorite shades. Printer's ink comes in tubes and is available in oil-base and water-soluble. Water-soluble is better suited for school use because after the session the linoleum blocks, room, and children can be scrubbed with water instead of with turpentine. The ink is squeezed on to the glass palette and spread out with the brayer until it is evenly distributed and slightly tacky. When it is tacky, it is ready for use. If monochrome prints are made it is a good idea not to use straight black, since it is harsh and unattractive. Black mixed with sepia and blue becomes a rather beautiful tone. The colors that are squeezed onto the glass don't have to be mixed carefully. They mix themselves both on the brayer and on the linoleum. The print is actually more attractive when there are variations of tones.

The children stand around the big production table. Some get the paper ready, cutting it into the right sizes (about an inch all around wider than the linoleum cut to be printed). Others can grab the finished prints and lay them out to dry. Since every one is eager to do the actual printing, the teacher has to decide who goes first. The child who cuts the linoleum doesn't necessarily have to be the one who prints it. The teacher also has to watch that only small amounts of inks are squeezed on the glass, squeezing being an irresistible temptation.

There'll be some students who are better at particular phases of printmaking than others. Some will be instant experts on the correct tackiness of the ink, others who can measure and cut paper neatly. Each child will get constant advice from the onlookers as he performs his job—encouragement, discouragement, cheers, and boos:

"The ink is too wet!"

"Too dry man!"

"The paper moved while you printed!"

"That looks like an amoeba!"

"Yeah! A retarded one!"

"It's upside down!"

"Stupid, it doesn't matter. You just turn the paper around!"

"You can also stand on your head and look at it!"

"You stink. Let me do it!"

In other words, printmaking is a real assembly-line group activity, and, as mentioned, the only one advocated in this guide. I feel, in fact, inconsistent and apologetic for advocating it at all. An art-oriented group activity seems a contradiction in terms, since art instruction is concerned with the individual. When I think of groups, I think of children shorn of their identity, just marching together. (I also think of the inevitable cliché that group activity "developes leadership" which only makes me think of the followers who are bound to be developed at the same time.) What justifies the activity described here is that in addition to being creative, it is production-oriented—

just as a theatrical group is both creative and production-oriented—yet offers opportunities for individual initiative.

The following four basic modes of printing are only suggested points of departure for the creative student and teacher alike. The modes described are not only adventurous outlets for the student, but their technical elements and instant results have a particular attraction for the comparatively new, and more and more frequent phenomenon, the mechanically-minded, creative/scientific child. Some of them will probably assist other children in the actual cutting of the prints, if not do them for them. Other mechanically-minded children who may or may not excel in art, will especially relate to the productivity, precision, and experimental techniques of the printing process itself.

Mode 1. Printing in its simplest and most direct form means spreading the ink on the block, then pressing the block against paper or the paper against the block. Mechanical presses exist but are superfluous for school use. The resulting print, lifted off the block, is the direct reversal of the cut. If twenty prints are made they will all be the same, varying only with the amount of ink used and how evenly it is distributed on the block. Variety can be created by printing on colored paper, or by using several colors of ink on one block. The paper can be hand colored before printing or the finished print can be hand-colored with watercolors. When prints are hand-colored with watercolor, the printing ink is liable to bleed, unless oil-based inks have been used.

Mode 2 . Another method is to lay thin paper on the inked block, and to stroke it lightly with your hand, enough to get an idea of the outline of the print through the paper. Then, with the bottom of a small glass jar or the top of a Zippo lighter, rub only some areas. By exerting different degrees of pressure you achieve different degrees of darkness and shadow-like gradations from white to gray to black. Depending on the thickness and quality of the paper the finished print can often be used from either side. One side will have softer edges than the other and its image will not be reversed.

Mode 3. In a third printing method, only a trace of ink is put or left on the block—just enough to hold very thin paper in place. The brayer is inked and rolled over the image. This is a fairly delicate operation because there has to be just the right amount of ink on the brayer in order to avoid smudges. Sometimes the brayer is rolled over more than once. Where there is resistance from the underlying linoleum block, the paper will be toned. Where an area has been cut away from the linoleum, no resistance is encountered and no ink is deposited on the paper. Edges are soft in this printing-through process, in which there is, of course, no reversal. The exciting element in this method is that mysterious forms will appear apparently from nowhere. On investigation the children will discover where they come from: where the brayer does not find resistance, the ink remains on the brayer and is not deposited on the paper. As it rolls along, this ink gets discharged elsewhere on the paper where resistance is found from the surface of the uncut block. This means that there suddenly appears, apparently out of nowhere, a dark form which is the exact replica of a light form elsewhere, creating a kind of echo and rhythm all its own. This printing-through method can be done with colored inks instead of black or brown. Several brayers with different colors can be used, or two colors can be picked up by one brayer. Not every print will be successful, but every print will be different. You can even use two different prints on one paper, perhaps one printed direct, the other through, perhaps superimposing a figurative print on a linear one. Another effective technique that works well with some designs is doing what one is not supposed to do: move the paper while printing, thus getting a double exposure.

Mode 4. This method returns to the first one, the direct print in black or a mixture of black, brown, and blue. However, printing is done on full-page colored magazine ads from publications done on newsprint. *The New York Times Magazine* is a treasure chest for such material. Glossy paper is not suitable. By printing over these ads, blocking out part of them with areas of black, each print is a complete surprise. Whatever was on the ad has been utterly transformed. Some prints come out great, some miserable. Eventually, the children become more and more experienced in choosing the right kind of ad and the right area to print on it.

The above four modes of printing make no claim to originality or finality. Any professional printmaker could make up a different, longer, equally valid, or better list. Suggestions like these cannot or should not be fully understood or appreciated until tried, and adapted to one's own style. Their purpose is solely to give an idea of the endless possibilities and to serve as points of departure.

5.
Presentation, Communication, Competition

Attitudes towards art vary from school to school depending on a variety of factors, budgets sometimes being the least of them. They range from genuinely art-oriented, to tokenism or to a complete misconception of the role of art in education.

When a teacher takes over the art program of a school, he may have to do more than just work with children. A priority is to find out whether exhibition areas exist beyond the walls of the actual art room—in auditoria, cafeterias, corridors, principals' offices, etc. If none exist, they must be created. The art teacher will have to explain (in diplomatic language) that an art program without public display areas isolates the art activity from the rest of the school and nullifies art's purpose—to communicate feelings and ideas. Under such conditions the art instructor would indeed function in what amounts to a private world which he alone would have to carry and sustain. Though results may be valuable, such unrelated activity is not only unhealthy, but will, in the long run, tend to compensate for its isolation by encouraging eliticism and snobbery and end up alienated.

It is not enough that the teacher constitutes a receptive audience for the children's art within the familiar setting of the art room. The arts seek to communicate. The actual formal display of their work fulfills the children's need to reveal and to communicate. *This is an integral part of the creative process.* Public display of a child's piece provides the forum for communication as well as a confirmation of the validity of his work. Well-designed, frequently changed exhibitions of a few pieces only—so that they can be seen well—are an essential part of an art program.

Apart from improving the image of the school as a whole, these displays also show (in this age of accountability) what the teacher does and where he stands.

Exhibitions should, where possible, be in glass cases deep enough to accommodate sculptures and masks as well as paintings. There could be a "picture of the week" showcase which may, at times, puzzle and provoke the staff.

In addition to showcases, the children's work should, as a matter of course, be displayed on the walls of the art room itself. Work should not be tacked up; it should be dignified by being mounted properly. Sculptures should have bases. There is no painting or doodle that does not get transformed and improved by proper presentation. The most effective way is to cut mats for each piece. Dry-mounting is an alternative and can be done without much special equipment. A hot iron will do the job. Dry mounting preserves paintings and facilitates storage. Only older and well-coordinated children can be involved in the cutting of mats, since the knife used for cutting can be lethal.

A special area could also be provided in the art room for well-mounted reproductions, clippings, etc. which the teacher happens to like because they express his personal tastes or have aesthetic or thought-provoking qualities, say, a well-designed automobile, an early American wheelbarrow, Picasso's sculpture of babboon with toy-car head, or Magritte's man with the floating apple. There's a Herb Smit photograph of an egg on dark background. It beats all else for perfection, beauty, function, impact, and originality, and is a shining example of less being more—of economy. I feel no art room should be without it.

It is a good idea to get the children themselves involved in the planning, designing, and hanging of exhibits, to challenge them to come up with new and effective ideas. There is no reason why school corridor exhibits should not compare with museum exhibits in presentation and distinction.

Occasionally misguided corporations will arrange painting competitions and send notices to the principals of schools who will pass them on to the art teacher. Such competitions are best ignored. Competition may be part of life but that kind of competition does not belong in schools' art programs.

An art room that is concerned with the production of work of intrinsic artistic value is, in fact, no fertile ground for any kind of competition. When a really good piece of sculpture is admired, it is the sculpture that is admired, not the sculptor. When the teacher says "wow" the other children will sit up and look at the piece of work that provoked the "wow," not at the child who made it. Other children may examine their own work more closely, compete with themselves so to speak, in order to produce something that may provoke a wow reaction, too. If the teacher has established himself as someone who is sincere, honest, and selective in his criticism, and concerned with art, a competitive situation simply will not arise. In fact, children will take actual pride in the work of their peers. Where no material rewards are given for good work, the work becomes its own reward.

This goes for grading art work as well. The advent of teachers' "accountability," unaccountably coincides with the gradual abandonment of grades for students. Art has pioneered quite a few liberal practices which have been incorporated into teaching generally. Art teachers who put the art experience above results, always have opposed grading work—or have preferred to mark for effort rather than performance. In fact, where results do become important, poor performance in art can denote the teacher's rather than the student's failure.

The production of a group mural for public display, is also its own reward, if for no other reason than the impact of its sheer size. As mentioned earlier, mural painting is not a group activity, but rather a series of coordinated individual efforts, in which peer stimulation admittedly plays a part. If the children do not come up with a workable idea for such a mural, all the teacher really has to do is draw, say, a horizontal line across the center of the panel and say, "this is the ground, this is the sky," and each child can put in whatever he can do best—hills, rivers, houses, cars, people, trees, dogs, etc. Very popular and dramatic is a curved line which becomes the surface of the moon with the black space above. It lends itself to a great variety of outrageous space monsters, space ships, rockets, flying saucers, even signs that say things like 'verboten.' Murals are best first drawn in charcoal by individual students and painted in later, not necessarily by the same children. If there is a child who is good at shading he can eventually go over all the figures and make them look three-dimensional. He must be sure to choose one position for the supposed source of light so all the shadows go in the same direction.

There is a purist and an aesthetic school of thought on the cropping of children's work for the purpose of matting and exhibiting. I belong to the aesthetic school. Sometimes only part of a painting is good and would make a stunning piece. One can either cut the bad part off or cut the mat so that only the good part shows. Sometimes cropping transforms a mediocre piece into something sophisticated and surprising. Some pieces can be improved by being turned upside down, or by being tilted. Though this may be deemed entirely dishonest, and probably is, it can be a very useful tool in giving a less successful child a sense of achievement, even if, at first, he may not recognize the piece as his own. The question whether cropping is creative (which it is) or dishonest is irrelevant, as long as it promotes both the child's confidence and the artistic level of public displays.

The drawings, paintings, and sculptures by children reproduced here are a random selection of work considered honest and of artistic merit.

1. Clay. (*Robert C., age 12*)
2. Clay, sprayed with ink. (*Paul T., age 13*)
3. Clay, burnished and rubbed with furniture polish and cigarette ashes. (*Alan, age 15*)
4. Clay, sprayed with black paint. (*Frank, age 11*)
5. Clay, sprayed with ink. (*Paul T., age 13*)
6. Linoleum print. (*Richard, age 12*)
7. Ink, applied with brush. (*Billy S., age 12*)
8. Ink and wash. (*Billy S., age 10*)
9. Mascoid, watercolor applied with brayer. (*Michael L., age 14*)
10. Yoshi pen and ink. (*Judy, age 15*)
11. Pen and ink. (*Michael L., age 12*)
12. Pen and ink. (*Andre Z., age 11*)
13. Pen and ink. (*Andre Z., age 15*)
14. Charcoal. (*Jack, age 12*)
15. Watercolor. (*Robert C., age 12*)
16. Colored inks. (*Frank, age 12*)
17. Postercolor. (*David K., age 12*)
18. Watercolor. (*Anne, age 14*)
19. Ink and wash on brown paper. (*Ron., age 13*)
20. Watercolor. (*Gene, age 13*)
21. Ink and watercolor. (*David R., age 15*)
22. Crayon. (*George, age 10*)
23. Watercolor. (*Michael, age 12*)

1.

2.

3.

4.

5.

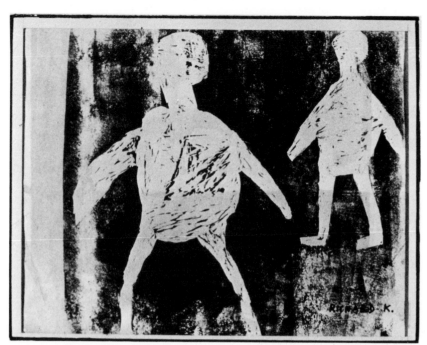

6.

7.

8.

9.

10.

11.

12.

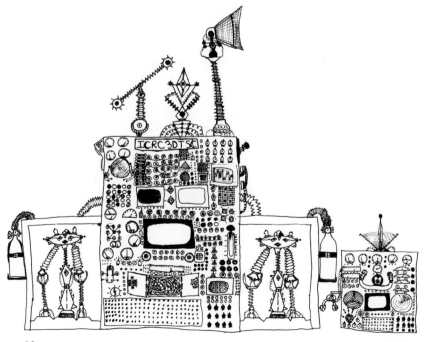

13.

14.

15.

16.

17.

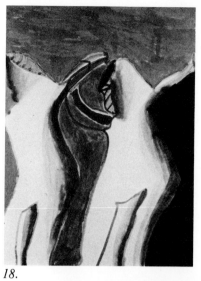

18.

20.

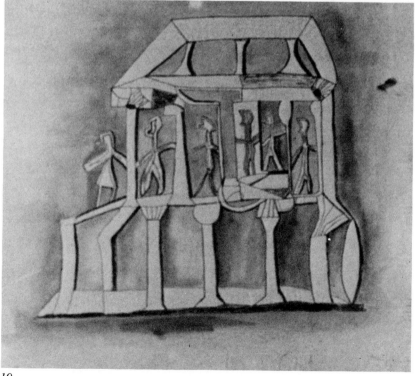

19.

21.

22.

23.

6.
Art and the Emotionally Disturbed Child

There is hardly a school that does not have a sprinkling of disruptive children. Some may be hyperactive, some merely exuberant, some may be emotionally disturbed. The latter have the advantage over the quietly troubled child who even in bona fide treatment centers tends to get overlooked and untreated until he starts smashing window panes.

Instead of considering tranquilizers, the conscientious art instructor may feel that a knowledge of art-therapy techniques would help him to help these children. When he investigates the literature on the subject—at times inspiring, at times highly specialized, at times a litany of case histories—he realizes that art therapy is as much an attitude to be taken as it is an art and/or science, and that there are as many approaches as there are ways of washing dishes. The approach depends on the personal inclinations of the therapist and on the setting where the therapy is practiced—just as the size and form of a sink will determine the method used in dishwashing.

Even with individual differences, art therapy can be said to fall into three main schools of thought:

1) Diagnostic-Psychological Orientation: The patient's work is used to diagnose his pathology.

2) Verbal Psychotherapeutic Orientation: The therapist encourages the patient to verbalize problems that become apparent in his work, then helps him overcome them through discussion.

3) Art Orientation: This works on the theory that art itself (rather than the therapist) heals, that the very act of painting is therapeutic (like dishwashing), and that the optimum situation is one where art becomes a symbolic act and, more than the statement of a problem, its sublimation and resolution.

Inevitably, the diagnostic therapist says that the art-oriented therapist is not a therapist at all, but an art teacher—who, in turn, feels "Art" has nothing to do with what the diagnostician does. The art-oriented therapist also feels that verbalization inhibits spontaneity of art expression by causing self-consciousness that interrupts the flow of creativity and is bound to result in repeating subject matter in order to prove a point.

As it must have become apparent, the art-oriented approach is the one favored here. It is the most accessible, self-contained, and the most obviously suited for an art program which deals with a limited number of disturbed or disruptive children, perhaps borderline or not diagnosed cases. Some children come from disrupted or broken families, thus lacking the supportive structure a home and family can provide; others may never have been exposed to the formative forces and values of tradition, culture, or religion.

For these students, art can fill a vacuum few other experiences can. The media are mastered easily, painlessly, in fact, joyously. Successful work and positive feedback—often what such children need most—are readily achieved. And there is this intangible called "art" to believe in. . . .

If the teacher's own enthusiasm for art rubs off, the alchemy of art will develop into a cult. Concern with the self will be superseded by a primary concern with art—eliminating that period of self-indulgence often experienced by people in therapy.

As far as the actual art work and the day-to-day dealings with these children are concerned, the difference between them and regular children is only one of degree—and the word "crucial" best describes its nature. An outspoken student/teacher relationship of some kind—even an embattled one—is *important* in any teaching situation, *necessary* when teaching art, *crucial* in art therapy. It has to be nurtured carefully. In fact, at least in the beginning it is more important for the child to relate to and trust the teacher and to feel wanted and at home in the art room than that he produces—although successful productions are often what cements such relations. Giving the child responsibilities, like having him issue materials, is a time-honored device every new generation seems to want to fall for. If the child has some special skills, such as, say, knowing how to use compasses, let him teach others. However, he should never receive preferential treatment he or others could interpret as special treatment and should be expected to behave, perform, clean up, etc. like everyone else. Formality and decorum are particularly important since his aggressions and emotions should be captured by his work rather than wasted in destructive behavior. Having played the role of the enfant terrible for some time, he will appreciate being just one of the guys.

Though most methods teachers use in a regular art class will work equally well as part of the therapeutic approach, situations may arise that tend to be precarious. A line drawn, a word dropped, can be critical. The fabric of the child's mind is tenuous. Timing, particularly, is critical: the child must be ready for whatever experience is brought to him. If the timing is right it can be a moment of truth. If not it can at best be meaningless, at worst frightening or disturbing. Even praise, badly timed, can be a turn-off. Troubled children who do outstanding work which is recognized as such, praised and treasured by the teacher, may at times destroy it for a variety of reasons. It may be that the message contained in the piece is not heeded, or because he wants to play games, get attention, see the teacher's reaction. Life is not easy for such children.

Recipes for such situations are both impossible to give and impossible to follow. What counts is that the instructor maintains an awareness of the therapy aspect of his work. The teacher will still be himself, but his spontaneity will be tempered with purpose. It is for his own sake, for his amour propre, for his objectivity, at times for his survival, that he maintain this awareness of the role he is playing: *No matter how rough (or smooth) the going, the teacher must never make a personal issue out of what occurs between the child and himself.* For the emotionally disturbed child he is a projection. It is this projection, not the man, the child addresses when he tells him he loves him or when he tells him—often in four-letter language—what to do with himself.

It may, or may not, be a good idea for the teacher to obtain data on the child's background. This is something he has to decide for himself. It might help him to understand and deal better with the child, or it may hinder his spontaneity, blunt his common sense, or, worse, make him an amateur psychiatrist. A creative instructor may just want to accept the child for what he sees in him and take it from there. But where cases puzzle, or cause concern, or seem difficult to reach, seeking information or even help from the social worker may be the wiser course.

Generally speaking, teaching responsively in a structured class applies here equally and follows the same development described earlier—doodle, experimentation, acquisition of skills, achievement, self-revelation. Each phase, including resulting failures and successes, becomes crucial, at times critical, when the emotionally disturbed child is involved.

As stated, recipes are impossible to give or to follow, but there *is* one for situations that the teacher does not know how to handle: *When in doubt, do nothing!* That, too, can be—but rarely is—a mistake.

7.
Evaluation and the Creative Process

One of the World's Fairs had a computer that made rather fair graphological analyses of samples of handwriting. No doubt, there will be, one day, computers that will teach people how to make original oil paintings and how to appraise and evaluate them. Educational analysts, theoreticians, and consumerists, similarly, look for precise data that can be categorized, computerized, and inserted into slots. Their hair would stand on end if they saw the kind of sloppy, personal, erratic, and subjective manner performance is being evaluated in the creative art situation, whether by the teacher or the student himself.

The ingredients of a painting, of course, *can* be categorized. A painting can be well-composed, intelligent, emotional, skillful, sincere, and/or economic. Yet, having all these qualities, it can still be bad. On the other hand, a painting can have just one of these qualities and be moving. It can be highly skillful and very bad or very good, can be awkwardly, clumsily done and be utterly beautiful.

The teacher, knowing more about the child, his work, and his potential, than the child himself, and having been involved in the evolution of the piece, cannot really be objective. He may reject a piece that another teacher or artist would think exquisite, admire another piece that his colleague would find commonplace.

Another kind of evaluation—response—takes place when work is exhibited. That particular evaluation is not very articulate or meaningful, since art is, or is becoming, more and more the domain of artists, and the non-artist no longer trusts himself to make judgments. Those who do, make judgments that can be pragmatic, associative, irrelevant, or ad hominem. Some of them, of course, "know what they like. . . ."

As for self-evaluation by students, it is an ongoing, integral part of the creative process and of the creative and personal growth of the student. At first the young artist has to rely entirely on the teacher's judgment. If he does something he knows or thinks is good, he isn't sure until he is told. He also takes cues from the teacher by watching his reaction to the work of fellow students. Since the taste of the instructor is, hopefully, catholic, children who work for immediate approval become confused: the teacher likes things that are carefully rendered, a minute later approves of a wild smear. He likes carefully planned as well as purely accidental work. He may reject a picture that seems really cute, almost as nice as things you see in magazines, yet admires another one that looks "corrodiated" and reminds you of death. It is a puzzlement.

Only after the child realizes that instead of trying to please the teacher, he should just be doing his own thing—he will have arrived.

Children, like adult painters, will, of course, try to repeat their successes. These will turn out to be sterile and lack the strength of the original. However, by the time they have chalked up enough successes, they will be secure enough to take risks and eventually get to the point where they paint for the need and pleasure of it. At this stage the child may go through an experience of awe, almost shock, (similar to one adult artists occasionally encounter) when he suddenly realizes that he is in the process of creating something that is so good and strong that it goes beyond himself, that he has created something that has a life of its own. Evaluation, or self-evaluation, becomes irrelevant at that point. Such things cannot be measured.

More than actual evaluation also takes place when a child is shown a painting he completed months earlier, highlighting another aspect of art: Meaningful work by growing children, like dreams that are quickly forgotten, is tied to a current experience. The painting thus belonged to a phase of his development that has been completed and is part of an experience the painting itself may have helped him to digest. He has outgrown that phase and, moving on, rejects the reminder: children do not look back. "*I* did that?! he will say, in disbelief.

8.
Discipline and the Teacher/Student Relationship

The "established" teacher does not have behavior problems in his classes. "Established" ipso facto denotes that his relationship with his students is either good, or has been resolved in some manner, perhaps through fear. Some teachers resort to a relationship based on fear because the student body requires it or because it fulfills needs the teacher has.

If a teacher continues to have discipline problems in his classes over a period of, say, ten years, he is either in the wrong profession or a masochist in the right profession.

A teacher on his first assignment trying to survive in a blackboard-jungle type situation and seeking solutions may find any answer glib. Obviously, for conditions depending on a great many factors, including the teacher's personality, aspirations, sensitivities, there are no pat answers. If conditions are such that he has to brace himself before entering the classroom, it may be that a decisive number of his students have characteristics that belong into the category described in Chapter 6, a re-reading of which might prove helpful.

Most problems in behavior control are faced by teachers who are either new and inexperienced or who are new at a particular school.

The art teacher, unless he presides over a free workshop where attendance is voluntary, faces the additional paradox of having to force students to be free and creative. For him to be a disciplinarian would be a contradiction in terms, yet he will be unable to function unless he asserts his authority at least in the beginning, or unless he happens to be very much in tune with the teacher who preceded him. He cannot enforce instant allegiance, but he can insist on good manners and general decorum. Since good manners are really more important than good art, and since children do not always learn good manners at home, the art teacher may have to begin by teaching manners—simple things like "closing" instead of slamming doors, or saying "good morning" when they come into the room. What "discipline" (a word that evokes Dickensian canes) really means is the enforcement of self-discipline, in other words, good manners. Les manières sont une forme qui simule la bonté et qui finit par la créer. (Manners are a form that simulates goodness and that ends up by creating it.) The teacher may have to go through a long period of patient insistence on such formalities until he can even think of functioning successfully as an art instructor. He will need to maintain a stubborn politeness for as long as it takes for good manners to rub off on the last child. Whoever is stubborn longer wins.

Though it is not quite clear what comes first, teacher/student relationships or good manners, you cannot have one without the other. "Conviction" is the key word in establishing either. Conviction does not have to be expressed in words. If it's there, it'll show. If the teacher maintains a no-nonsense, we-are-here-to-work attitude it will come across that he's simply too busy to bother with silly little attempts at disruption. The fun is taken out of disruptions when nobody reacts to them. The teacher's conviction should cover not only art, but manners, cleanliness, and working habits. Once these have been formed, the children themselves will share the teacher's desire to work in a peaceful atmosphere. *They* will be the ones to discourage disturbances.

Individual children act differently when in a group. Classes tend to have a group character of their own, conditioned by a number of factors, such as constellation of students, pecking order, and approach, attitude, and mentality of their regular teacher. Groups are, of course, more difficult to handle than individual children, unless one is geared to them, which the art teacher is not. Art-oriented people harbor an aversion to groups. The art room especially is the place where children can get away from groups and become individuals. It is quite possible to have relationships with individual children, yet have trouble with a group of them. This becomes critical only in the beginning and at the end of each period, since by seating arrangements, the nature of the work, etc., groups are broken up during the actual session. There is, therefore, not much the art teacher can do in those few weekly sessions (apart from getting them interested) but make sure they know who is the boss. It's a recognized technique: strictness at first, gradual relaxation as strictness becomes superfluous. Only the starry-eyed idealist will start out permissive, only to end up screaming. There are all sorts of techniques to ease the transition from entering the class to settling down to work. One is the surprise announcement or joke. One that has some shock value because it is the opposite of what is usually done or expected is to sit at one's desk when the children come in and say: "Don't bother me. I'm working. Walter, would you give the students their material and help them?" The kids will peep at what you're painting and tip-toe to their seats. When someone is noisy, the other students will yell (far too loudly), "shut up, we're working."

The "work" the teacher is doing brings up the question: how much should the children know about the teacher's own work if he happens to be an artist? Since his own knowledge and ability is part of his work, there is no reason why the children shouldn't know about it. The question of "influencing" them might be raised by a purist, but is irrelevant at the elementary-school age. It may become relevant only at college level. Young children are bound to be influenced anyway, since it is the teacher who councils them, picks their work, judges it, exhibits it, etc. The teacher's abilities are also his tool kit in establishing himself. In fact, if he is, say, good at portraits (and even if he isn't), he can use that as a powerful weapon to establish relationships with recalcitrant or alienated children by asking them to pose for him. It takes two to make a portrait and the model must do part of the work by sitting still. Looking into each other's eyes during the fifteen minutes or so the sketch may take can be an experience. It is "relating" of the quality two people experience when they sing together. Something else will happen: as the model is being scrutinized and put down on paper, he will undergo a change. Distrust and bitterness will vanish. He will simply become a child who is being given attention. The secret, of course, is the time and attention given. These are the most valuable gifts a child can receive.

Among the children who relate to you, there will be two extremes: those who identify with you and those who fight you. The student who identifies with you, emulates you, is obviously the easier one to handle, more comfortable, even useful since he'll always be delighted to take over some of your duties. He obviously has a need to identify with a symbolic figure at this time of his life and the art teacher happened to be there to fulfill that need. (It could easily have been the football coach or the garbage collector—just to put things into perspective so that the art instructor's inflatable ego won't pop.)

The other extreme, the youngster who fights the teacher, relates to him just as strongly, but uses him differently. Basically, he probably has more on the ball than the passively accepting student. He may, in fact, get more out of the teacher than the one who identifies with him. While fighting, or questioning, he will still absorb what is taught. He may say green when the teacher says red, but with his need to find his own answers he demonstrates a more valuable and creative way to learn, no matter how miserable he makes life for the teacher.

Everyone feels the need to rebel at one time in his life. The formative teens are the best time to do it in and to get it over with. The conforming youngster will inevitably rebel later. He may rebel by dropping out of college, breaking up a family, etc. Rebellion during the teenage years seriously affects only the child; rebellion later in life may affect his career or a lot of other people, who may be the ones to pay the price.

Teenage rebellion is not something a teacher should try to quell or soften. In fact, unless it gets too rough, he should feed it and stimulate it (without being provocative) until it has run its course. A conciliation, call to "reason" should not be forced. The rebel himself will determine the end of the rebellion.

The needs of teachers (who have needs, too) are usually met by their students' positive response to their teaching. When a particular student responds and relates to the art teacher to the point of identification, regarding him as the maestro who can do no wrong, he becomes the ideal student. His attitude is one that is hard to accept casually.

In practice, in the case of non-parents of either sex, who have picked the teaching profession in the first place because of their dedication and capacity to give, such gratifying relations are not always as casually accepted as they should be. This is worth discussing at a time when more men enter professions like social work and primary education, fields previously restricted to women, and where ambivalent responsibilities are forced upon them. An art instructor, on his first assignment, may misinterpret his role, become overinvolved with a devoted pupil whose work also is outstanding. He may unconsciously become protective, possessive, reach the point of transference of his paternal/maternal instincts and lose sight of the fact that the child's choice of him as a model is coincidental.

His real role in the child's growth and development must be fitfully limited in place (art room), time (Tuesdays from 2–3), and scope (art education). If extended beyond those limits it can indeed hinder or distort rather than advance the child's natural development.

Restraint is particularly appropriate in therapeutic situations described in Chapter 6, where emotional involvement can be precarious and reach sudden critical mass.

9.
Inequality and the Talented Child

Embarrassed by the fact that we are all born unequal, educators use a variety of euphemisms to describe or to deny the existence of children that are stupid.

Now that *that* taboo has been violated, let us say that given the right environment (which it is the teacher's responsibility to provide) art is the one area where a "mentally impaired," even a borderline retarded child, functioning strictly at his own level, can do outstanding work of intrinsically high caliber, even if not consistently.

Nature has given to many a "developmentally disabled" child a wonderfully compensatory gift: unerring, stubborn goal-consciousness. An art instructor can council, influence, make suggestions to the intelligent child, but not to the "low I.Q." one. The "mentally handicapped" knows where he is going. What is most surprising, the wrong color, used over your protest, will often turn out to be the right color.

Intelligence may be the ability to select the essential, but the "slow-learning" young artist is often able to get right down to basics— where even the intelligent adult may get side-tracked by non-essentials, frequently arriving at basics only through a process of patient elimination.

There are certain recurrent somatotypes that are worth mentioning since every teacher is likely to encounter them. They will not be as cut-and-dried and black-and-white as described here. There is the high I.Q. child who is good at everything, including art. Although he will produce outstanding art work for a while, his involvement will be temporary since his intellectual curiosity will soon lead him into new areas of endeavour. There will be the child with fully developed middle-class values—a protective cover hard to break and which, perhaps, should not be broken. The art teacher, after all, cannot affect the whole world. There will almost certainly be the inarticulate introvert. He may be inarticulate because of his true respect for language, which is why the inarticulate are, at times, capable of an eloquence all their own. They often manage to express emotions in painting, that cannot be put into words. These children, as well as their work, are often interesting, valuable, and worth watching.

Then, of course, there is the "talented" child. Talent comes in two sizes. One is the true artistic talent which, for our purposes, we shall call the "gifted" child to differentiate him from the child with a facility.

The child with a facility for drawing is the most hopeless and frustrating student an art teacher can have, partly because the accepted objectives of a creative art class are impracticable for him. He usually comes fully developed. He may be influenced by comic-strip characters. His drawing will be realistic though slightly simplified or schematic. He can draw anything he puts his mind to. A ham, he uses art as showmanship; his work is always visual (rather than haptic); his hero, naturally, is Dali. He likes approval and cannot take criticism. He's kind of pathetic because he thinks he's terrific, and often is. He's sensitive, too, and it would break one's heart to say anything to him that might prick his balloon. Such talent is often linked to a superficial and/or second-rate mind, as demonstrated by the fact that he cannot get beyond his facility. He functions best with facile media, like repetograph on smooth paper. One can attempt to give him other media, like a rough yoshi reed on rough or brown paper, so he has to fight his medium, slowing down his facility, giving more depth to his work. It won't last. He will eventually corrupt any medium, be slick even if he works with a broomstick. The best that can be done for such a youngster (and he will resist even that) is to let him draw from nature, let him study details, movements, hands, anatomy, perspective. This will give more substance to the otherwise schematic nature of his work and prepare him for what he can probably become one day: an excellent commercial artist—nothing to be sneezed at. His very accomplishment prevents him from trying anything new; he has a reputation to preserve and if experiments failed where would he be then? His very talent prevents him from growing. But he *can* perfect his style.

The "gifted" student, on the other hand, with a true talent for drawing and painting does have the potential for self-expression and growth. Sometimes, depending on his cultural background, he may get corrupted by parents and teachers before he gets to the seventh grade. With the urge to paint since early childhood, he would do the kind of thing he sees on the walls of his home, in books and magazines—pleasant little landscapes, sunsets, flowerpieces, what have you. He may even do Picasso-like images and call it "modern art." Encouraged by parents and teachers he may have been led to regard art as a social grace and may continue to do "safe" paintings rather than to experiment.

For this kind of student, finding an art tacher who opens the world of real art to him, will be an eye-opener and revelation. After that, there is not much such a child can or has to be taught—except one single concept. If he can accept that concept, he will be able to give up his safe little landscapes and begin to paint from his guts.

The concept: *Once you know how to do something, it's no longer worth doing.*

Index